Thieves Of Time Still Lose To Fate

You can love the stars, but you can't change them

Antranig Pathak

BookLeaf Publishing

India | USA | UK

Made with ❤ on the BookLeaf Publishing Platform

www.bookleafpub.in

www.bookleafpub.com

Dedication

To all the people who helped me experience love,

This one is for you.

Not all stories ended well, but this is proof that they are worth remembering.

Forever and always.

Yours truly,
Andy.

Preface

Dear Reader,

I have been lucky enough to experience love:

a rare and precious privilege, and one I do not take for granted.

I am still young, with much more to learn.

But here is what I can tell you:

This is what love feels like to me.

The poems in this book, in the order you find them, trace the stages of me falling in and out of love.

Along the way, this book weaves together many different love stories, bringing back memories I will always cherish.

As you turn these pages, I hope you find echoes of your own heart here too.

If you have known love, I hope you relive the highs.

And if you have not, I hope you experience it vicariously through me.

Yours truly,
Andy

Acknowledgements

Mom, thank you for safely keeping the first poem I ever wrote. Your endless support still makes me believe I can do just about anything.

Dad, thank you for blasting ghazals through the house my entire childhood. Somewhere between your playlists and your passion, I found the confidence to create, and to survive endless rewrites.

To Mahir, Ishika, Krishna, Kashvi, Jenny, Dev, Harsh Kedia, Najar, and Siya, thank you for putting up with my complete meltdown over choosing the book cover. Honestly, you're all saints. And beyond that, thank you for always hyping up my art like proud moms at a talent show. I love you for it.

Kadira, you are one of the most creative minds I have ever seen in action. Thank you for reminding me to keep honing my art.

Thank you to BookLeaf Publishing for giving me the platform to share my words and dreams with the world. I'm truly grateful for the opportunity.

And finally, thank you, Pinterest. Without your endless poetry prompts, this book might've just been one sad haiku and a doodle.

1. Moon Child

Luna, I am falling for a daughter of yours,
A moonbeam, divine and free from any flaws,
She's got every bit of your serene charm,
In her fingers is the blood of all that is calm.

Luna, she's just like you, radiating light,
The one with whom the oceans surrender to fight,
And she pulls them towards herself with ease,
She induces fierce beauty in all of the seas.

Luna, she illuminates the darkest of nights,
The blood in my veins answers to her eyes,
Her being of stardust makes the galaxy smile,
She is all that is pure in the night sky.

Luna, I swear her touch brings me alive,
The kind for which the men in war die,
I'm longing and craving for mercy like her,
But before I fall, I must know your answer.

Luna, I ask for her hand to be with me,
She is all the colour that makes me dream,
And my endless complaints to you about being lonely,
Have found one of your daughters to complete this story.

2. [11:11]

You're looking at the stars,
And I'm looking at you,
We've travelled to Mars,
And back to my house's roof.

I tear my eyes away,
I glance at the time,
The night is now awake,
11:11, a minute that's mine.

So I grin and close my eyes,
And wish for you then,
Even though you're by my side,
And this place is now heaven.

You ask why I'm hushed,
I stutter and try to stall,
You ask why I blushed,
And I can't breathe at all.

So I say that I'm making a wish
To which you laugh and say,
That you didn't ever think,
That I'd believe in fate.

I say I never did and don't,
But I think it's so serene,
A minute full of hope,
Where all lost souls can dream.

The minute is now over,
The stars are still the same,
My thoughts are now sober,
And nothing seemed to change.

But I'll wait another day,
Till this minute comes to me,
And I'll wish for you again,
Until you're mine to keep.

3. So, who was going to warn me?

So who was gonna warn me about the girl who loved the sea,
The one who pulled me into the waves and taught me how to breathe?
With fingers that slip into mine like that's where they were meant to be,
With lips singing 'Riptide', and hair that smells like the breeze.

And when the sun starts setting, her skin glows like the sky,
I guess that happens when the view adjusts to your eyes.
And when she kneels in the water, you'll lose all track of time,
Because all I did was wait for her hand to be back in mine.

When she's flirted with the sea, and she's back to the shore,
When she's showered, in her pajamas and drying her hair by the door,
I feel my heart skipping a beat because of all that we leave unexplored,

But as I hear her call my name, I'm confused about what
to say anymore.

Then we watched the genre of films that she got me to
like,
I find myself staring at her, and I'm drowning in her
eyes,
She's oblivious to my eyes, and how they're longing for
her to smile,
But she shifts close to me and puts her head next to
mine.

And there's silence for a while, because I don't know
what to do,
I want to kiss her, but I'm scared, and we're always just
confused.
I tuck her hair aside and wait, hoping to get a cue,
But that's impossible when the people waiting for a
signal are not one but two.

So who was gonna warn me about the girl who disarms
me with her smile?
The kind you fall in love with and enjoy the whole ride.
'Cause even fate gave up on pulling us apart this time,
We're just two people and a thread, and it's holding just
fine.

4. I'll say it someday

I'll say it someday, I swear,
But maybe I'm comfortable now,
If all of it was just out in the open air,
I'd still find a way to drown.

Because I wouldn't change a thing,
Not a second, nor a minute or day,
This is our story, just the beginning,
But it's been etched into stone for decades.

But that means it's forever, right?
Or at least something close to infinity?
And that means I'll find the perfect time,
And we'll forget that there was ever any misery.

I've woven the strings of fate,
I've burned my hands at the stars,
Until my destiny spelled out your name,
And all that's mine is ours.

I'll say it someday, I swear,
And I'll make sure you hear it loud,
Because I see it in the way you stare,
You're waiting for it all to work out.

5. Tujhe Kaise Pata Hoga?

Tujhe kaise pata hoga, mujhe naye cheezon ka darr hai?
Badlav se bechaini mujhe hoti aksar hai,
Kyunki jab tak main samjhun aur koshish jataun,
Sab badal jaata hai, aur main dukh farmaun.

Tujhe kaise pata hoga, mujhe naye logon ka darr hai?
Unko samajhne mein galti hoti aksar hai,
Aur agar woh mujhe na samjhe, toh kya karun?
Bas aise hi panno par dil ke lafz bharun?

Tujhe kaise pata hoga, tu inmein se nahi hai?
Tujhse darr toh door, mujhe muskurahat mili hai,
Aur ek naye shakhz ka darr chhup sa gaya hai,
Kyunki kuch bhi badle, tu sirf mera hai.

Tujhe kaise pata hoga, mujhme abhi bhi darr hai?
Tujhe khone ka khayal mujhe satata aksar hai,
Sab bhula ke main tujhme khona chahta hoon,
Har pal teri khoj mein, main sirf tera ban jaata hoon.

6. Pools of Honey

I've never been this obsessed quite soon,
Until my eyes met yours at noon,
A glowing horizon left me doomed,
A weird homeliness I found in you.

 A meadow at sunset, we're right there,
Pictures, kisses, dates all in a flare,
In my arms, I'll play with your hair,
Those eyes told me too soon that I care.

Shining glasses, magnified they looked,
Under a spell, I was just hooked,
An innocence you held in looks,
I'd only read this in books.

Oakwood ambers, I'm electrified,
I've seen us together in those eyes,
When you hold me in the darkest night,
Your pools of honey, I took a dive.

I swim against desire, holding tight,
A golden heaven in those eyes,
Every time they're on me, I'm high,
Your pools of honey make me smile.

Eye for an eye, the whole world goes blind,
And your pools of honey have stolen mine.

7. Oh, Aphrodite

Was I made for someone,
Or were they made for me?
I don't search for love,
But I feel it come for me.

And love became scary,
It hurt me time again,
And being lovers,
Was a reminder of the pain.

And when I sing this now,
Take this as a plea,
Or maybe just a request,
From somebody like me.

Oh, Aphrodite, I think I'm in love,
I've found somebody that makes me blush,
Someone to hold me when times get tough,
I can hear you laughing up above.

Oh, Aphrodite, an ex lover
Once said to me,
"Romanticism is nothing,
But loving desperately."

I disagree but still act,
Like all that's right,
If I feel desperate,
I'll ruin this love I like.

And when I sing this now,
Take this as a plea,
Or maybe just a request,
From somebody like me.

Oh, Aphrodite, I think I'm in love,
I've found somebody that makes me blush,
Someone to hold me when times get tough,
I can hear you laughing up above.

Keep this song from a lover alive,
Promise this fool that everything's fine,
Now that I can call someone mine,
I hope my heart doesn't have to break this time.

Oh, Aphrodite, I feel my soul ignite,
Oh, Aphrodite, I'm reminded of the sky,
Oh, Aphrodite, those eyes, they hypnotize,
Oh, Aphrodite, every part of me is alive.

If you're somewhere, listening above,

Let me show you what love does,
Intoxication in just one touch,
Oh, Aphrodite I think I'm in love.

8. Tu Mera Roz

Tu mera roz ban rahi hai,
Woh aadat jo hat ti nahi hai,
Ek aisa nasha jo deewana banaye,
Ek aisa raag jo paas bulaye.

Tu mera roz ban rahi hai,
Woh khwaab jo khushi bharti hai,
Ek aisi roshni jo mujhe pehchaane,
Ek safar jo mujhe banjaara banaye.

Tu mera roz ban gayi hai,
Woh duniya jahan sab sahi hai,
Ek kinaara jahan saagar lehrati hai,
Aur ambar ki aankhon mein chamakti hai.

Tu mera roz ban gayi hai,
Ek aisi shakhz jo sirf meri hai,
Ek taara jo mere peeche hi rahe,
Jiski baat mujhse chaand bhi kare.

9. Made Me For You

I still wash my hair on Wednesdays and Sundays,
Just like my first 'girlfriend' told me she did.
I still hear the ocean, the sound of the waves,
Just like the first girl I loved when I was a kid.
I still sit on the merry-go-round and laugh,
One of my girlfriends loved the thrill of the rush,
I still break my Oreos into two halves,
Because someone who did it was a crush.
I still listen to Billy Joel, feeling something sweet,
Because of an ex who loved the old tunes,
I hold on to "The Night We Met,"
A song that echoes in my heart and swoons.
I don't love any of them anymore,
But they're parts of the things I do,
And darling, the only reason they matter,
Is because they made me likable to you.
They made me so I was made for you,
They left their stubborn little marks,
And before you think I'm feeling blue,
It's only because we are apart.
The past can only hold water,
If you deem it fit for you,
And darling, they wouldn't matter,
If they didn't break me down for you.

10. Zikr Toh Karo

Zikr toh karo,
Mohtarma, hum intezaar karenge,
Tum zidd toh karo,
Tumhaare saath baadal bhi ruthenge.

Mauka toh do,
Ki hum khwaaishein puri kar denge,
Sauda kar lo,
Har gehraai mein rang bhar denge.

Apni ada se ruthna,
Humaara dil tarsa jaayega,
Humaari baahon ko dhoondhna,
Aur humaari rooh lalchaayegi.

Apni aankhon se tum,
Bas humaari dhadkano ko daudana,
Apni zulfon se tum,
Mere zehen ki raaton ko sajaana.

Bas maang lo,
Is duniya mein aisa kya chhupa,
Jo hum lakhon-croreon,
Main se ek ko bhi na mila?

Agar tum mil gayi,
Toh bhala kya na mile?
Agar tumse hi bani,
Toh kaunsi baat na ban jaaye?

Zikr toh karo,
Mohtarma, bas ek pal bacha lo,
Faisla kar lo,
Aur iss dil ko sambhaal lo.

11. Love and War

Ares:
The blood of war is my glass of wine,
The lust for blood pulses through my insides,
But no one makes my heart race in speed
Like the curves of your hips and eyes so deep.
Even war could not corrode a being like you,
Aphrodite, my love, you're a breathtaking view,
And no one could ever calm my veins,
Your love is worth every war that's waged.

Aphrodite:
I'm sorry the blood on your lips is not mine,
But only love makes wars that threaten mankind,
Love can corrode; you underestimate the dues,
Of falling in love, with the dangerous hues,
Ares, my love, my injustice often exceeds yours,
Hearts broken in love hurt more than death in wars,
So, who could get you going, if not me?
Love and war have never done anything justly.

So, there you go, reader, the personification's clear:
Love is seldom fair and war is seldom dear,
Only the heavens could make this match because,
All is fair in love and war.

12. Ancient Names

Songs of the eras, they whisper names,
In the boundless waters and their waves,
Yet they're loud and consume the sky,
An ancient name, the first one in time.

And this being lives in the depths of my seas,
Gazing at me, teaching me how to breathe.
Awakening the syllables of love from slumber,
Rummaging the sky with lust and thunder,
With the power to bend the wills of men,
And eyes that compete with the light of heaven,
Labyrinths of thoughts all lead to her face.

I try but the words never seem to find a place,
My thoughts are lost in time forever and long.

I'll hide their muses and letters in this song,
Now retelling the folklore that made it to this dawn.

Let her in; I want her to see it all as is,
Over the mountains of obsession, a void exists
Vast realms of loneliness, longing an ancient name
Every second, every eternity, it's doomed to wait.

Why, if I must, I shall speak my truth to the stars,
If you're still looking at me, you'll hear the demands,
Then decide for yourself, if the songs are meant to be,
Having danced in their tunes before this eternity.

Yet as tempting as it is, the realities have changed,
Only the comets could align to fix our broken fate.
Unless we take the strings in our hands and intertwine
the tales.

13. Cadence

Draw me in, speak in perfect cadence,
Late-night musings, I'm contemplating.
The clock's hands race; I get impatient,
Knife on my neck, the blade's serrated.

Those eyes of yours, your perfect cadence,
Heavy breathing, cruising through stages.
You smile like you know I'm worth saving,
"Never loved you more", that's such an understatement.

Freestyle moments, your luring cadence,
Drop the knife, forget your motivations.
You're thinking while our past is congregating,
Run away with me? I'll be waiting.

You slipped, got caught up in my cadence,
I know you even in your imagination,
Blade's in my hand now, I'm just playing,
My offer's still up, I'll be by the pavement.

Walking down, I can feel you shaking,
Thinking about everything we're chasing,
Jump out the window; we're just wasted,
Speak to me in your perfect cadence.

14. Hades and Persephone

On the throne of the bones of my past lovers,
I saved a seat for a woman like you.
And though the earth now yields its colours,
Hades has Persephone and I have you.

The red of the pomegranate is still on your teeth,
Yet the cloth that drapes you is starting to glow
I seem to have forgotten that you were a borrowed queen,
The seasons are changing, your time has come to go.

My words command the underworld of my heart,
But they couldn't possibly hold you back for me,
These halls will feel lonely when we are apart,
But I promised that I would let you leave.

The Styx is now stirring, she's a bad replacement,
She couldn't fill the void of a companion like you,
Cerberus is bored, he's lost all his amazement,
The darkest place somehow has a darker hue.

But the world calls you, and this world is mine,
Only some time is what we were allowed to choose,

And I'll spend each second undoing the intertwined,
Hades had Persephone and I had you.

15. Substance Abuse

It's the taste of your lips,
Highs when we kiss,
Infatuation .
Craving for another drink,
Searching for bliss,
Intoxication.

Just like puffs in my lungs,
Nicotine turns me numb,
Neurotoxins.
With every stain on my tongue,
I cry when I'm done,
Oxytocin.

Addicted to love,
Cause you taste like a drug,
Or maybe I'm just never sober,
Manipulation and bluff,
But it's never enough,
Cause the cravings don't get over.

You taste like alcohol,
Then mess with my mind,
Not saying it was your fault,

But gosh, you weren't right.
You taste like everything,
That makes me feel high,
Morphine and Heroin,
Slowly kill me inside.

It's the smell of your coat,
Like fresh weed in a roll,
Domination.
Every breath, with a smoke,
You're the tar in my throat,
Contemplation.

Addicted to love,
Cause you taste like a drug,
Or maybe I'm just never sober,
Manipulation and bluff,
But it's never enough,
Cause the cravings don't get over.

You taste like alcohol,
Then mess with my mind,
Not saying it was your fault,
But gosh, you weren't right.
You taste like something so,
Neat, I feel so divine,
Then when the dosage goes,

I'll hurt some more inside.

Why do you taste so sweet,
But poison me inside?
Why can't I let you be,
And crave another high?
Why do you make me feel,
Like I'm in the sky?
Then when you make me weep,
I fall back to my life.

You taste like nights when,
You can't keep track of time,
When smoke and mirrors blend,
You'll leave me behind.

16. Crime Scene

The caution tape shines bright,
Broken hearts are what we left,
We'll run away, ready to hide,
We'll make it out before we're dead.

I'll try to say that I hate you,
But I'll stutter and take it back,
This tango always takes two,
Until the heart's under attack.

And now our bloody hands,
Show the damage we can do,
We'll try everything we can,
Till the other is guilty and sued.

Who knew words could kill?
They outdo what eyes can see,
Leave you hurt and broken amidst,
This love is now a crime scene.

It's better if I run away,
Don't wanna be caught so weak,
I'll admire it from where I'm safe,
This love is now a crime scene.

We'll toss the blame around,
And play the stupidest games,
While our stories stain the ground,
We'll come back to them someday.

And now our bloody hands,
Show the damage we can do,
We'll try everything we can,
Till the other is guilty and sued.

Who knew words could kill?
They outdo what eyes can see,
Leave you hurt and broken amidst,
This love is now a crime scene.

Act like I am a stranger,
Unlike the partners we've been,
Wait, you run away from danger,
This love is now a crime scene.

And when you find a new partner in crime,
I'll be there to remind you that you were once mine.

Run away, but you'll come back soon,
To pick up the evidence, you want it too,

Ex partners in crime meet eventually,
Remember, you can't stay away from me.

17. Envy

Call me envious, call me mad,
I am jealous, I am bad,
But it's only my agony at work,
Hey, I know it's kinda sad,
Longing for things I've never had,
Don't blame me; it's my heart that has been hurt.
I sin differently than you,
Can't I sin when my heart's blue?
You say envy turns my will to ash,
Who's to say I will not do,
The things that envy can induce,
If I go crazy, you wouldn't dare change that.

I envy things, not beings and souls,
I envy everything that holds,
A glimpse of your senses,
Oh, it makes me feel so helpless,

I envy the sheets you drape at night,
And the shirt that hugs you tight,
And the glass that touches your lips,
How do I envy all of this?
Why can't you be mine?
I envy your glasses all the time,

They can stare at your lonely eyes,
My love for you hasn't died,
Maybe I'll envy all my life.
Why can't I just feel alright?

Don't tell me you've never felt,
Envy for me, that won't help,
It's so new but that's what you fear,
Don't you miss touching my belt,
You gotta admit to it yourself,
You know that's all I wanna hear.

I envy things, not beings and souls,
I envy everything that holds,
A glimpse of your senses,
Oh, it makes me feel so helpless,

I envy the sheets you drape at night,
And the shirt that hugs you tight,
And the glass that touches your lips,
How do I envy all of this?
Why can't you just be mine?
I envy the mirror in your room,
It can always look at you,
The curtains that you touch,
Envy makes it all so much.

Why can't I be all right?

I think envy is misused,
It doesn't have to mean abuse,
When envy always has a muse,
Why isn't envy an art too?
I think envy can be meek,
Envy makes me feel so weak,
Maybe envy helps you see,
What you could never be.

I envy skies you smiled at too,
The stars you told the truth,
The drink you sin with,
I envy your absinthe,
Why can't you just be mine?
I envy the sheets you drape at night,
And the shirt that hugs you tight,
And the glass that touches your lips,
How do I envy all of this?
Why can't I just be all right?

18. Half a Minute

Break me inside.
Corrode the iron in my blood,
Look me in the eyes,
You know I crumble at your touch,
My bones ignite,
When your body's against mine.

Why do you stare?
Stare and don't dare say a word,
You know that you care,
Clear your throat but thoughts get blurred,
Your scent is in the air,
It's more than I can bear.

Half a minute died,
You turned around and left me,
Lost in my mind,
I can hear you grin when you leave,
You still watch the time,
To catch glances in the night.

Half a minute died,
Your bubblegum blue tongue is lonely,
Are you craving mine?

Turn and say that I'm your only,
I could spend the night,
Until we're satisfied.

Pinned against the wall,
Wouldn't we like that my darling?
Your lips say it all,
Who cares about ringing sirens?
Fix the wounds in salt,
No matter how small.

I miss your breath,
Miss your hands all over me,
Dive into the depth,
Make up for the time in between,
All you should expect,
Are my arms around your neck.

Half a minute died,
You turned around and left me,
Lost in my mind,
I can hear you grin when you leave,
You still watch the time,
To catch glances in the night.

Half a minute died,
It feels like everything is perfect,

When you're by my side,
Don't you dare leave me hurting,
With tears beneath my eyes,
Under this haunting sky.

19. Water Under the Bridge

Why'd you cut your hair?
It still looks good, I like it,
Why do I even care?
It's not in me to go spiting.

Why'd you switch your glasses?
New frames to watch me bleed?
Or are you entering the masses?
Bet you're scouting your next retreat?

Say what I wanna say?
I'd rather jump from this bridge.
You're not gonna go away?
When I needed you, you slipped.

If it's water under the bridge, why are we still drowning?
Why can't you let it go, why's my heart still pounding?
If it's water under the bridge, come take a swim,
We're in the flood, and the current wins.

Why'd I write this song?
To claw you from my brain.
Why'd you take so long?
You like driving me insane.

Why'd I call you back?
Your silence crushed my head.
Your words, just empty acts,
Lies that left me dead.

Say what I wanna say?
I'd rather jump from this bridge.
You're not gonna go away?
When I needed you, you slipped.

If it's water under the bridge, why are we still drowning?
Why can't you let it go, why am I still frowning?
If it's water under the bridge, come jump in,
I'd rather drown with you than call this a win.

20. Waves

Missing you comes in waves,
And tonight I'm drowning,
I fight the current, amazed,
As I see you frowning,
When my head goes underwater,
I feel your eyes stare,
Your gaze just gets hotter,
As I long for the salty air.

Missing you comes in waves,
And tonight, the tide is high,
If in the moment I can't be saved,
I'll drown scavenging for the moonlight,
And if that's all you wished to see,
Try jumping in, you'll realize,
The most beautiful thing you can do is save me,
And we'll swim our way out of this night,

My drowning is desperate and quiet,
But I see you notice all of it,
You couldn't help but smile,
Your sadism is astonishing,
Don't give me false hopes,
I've made it out alive a couple of times,

I've walked on thin tightropes,
With the pit of you raging on either side.

Missing you comes in waves,
I've drowned, it's dumb I know,
I've lost my willpower,
Oh lord just let me go,
I promised myself to stay,
But I guess the tide was strong,
At least I saw the light of day,
I had you all along.

21. You still keep the score

Running around in circles,
We won't quit playing games,
I think it's hardly fair,
Your rules always change,
I can't keep up anymore,
We'll never be the same.

I told myself for months,
That you've been this way,
I tried to tell you multiple times,
That lasted for a day,
Then we're back to normal,
Was I supposed to be okay?

I've been harsh up till now,
You were also good,
But there's this small thing,
I never understood.

If you know you've won, you've won,
Why still keep the score?
Why can't you be done, just done,
You make me hurt even more.

All we did was run, just run,
I'm crying on the floor,
This game we played was never fun,
But you still keep the score.

1-0, you forgot me,
That was just a start,
2-0, you're happy,
While I'm falling apart,
3-0, you can party,
Without missing my wretched heart.

You were amazing I think,
Not the best you could,
But there's this small thing,
I never understood.

If you know you've won, you've won,
Why still keep the score?
Why can't you be done, just done,
You make me hurt even more.

No reasons to talk, not one,
You're a stranger out of my door,
Everything we did can't be undone,
And you still keep the score.

Your score is a lot higher,
But I won't admit it,
I'd rather be quiet,
I haven't even scored,
I think I'll wing it,
Were you really just bored?

22. How Odd

How odd it is to be haunted,
By someone who is still alive,
To have a need to be wanted,
By a stranger you once liked,
And how weird it is to long for,
Someone who no longer exists,
And insane to write songs for,
The silhouette in the mist.

How odd it is to be haunted,
By the thing that made me smile,
The thing I once flaunted,
Now poisons my insides,
And how weird it is to crave,
Someone and not something,
To finally see through the haze,
Only to realize they're missing.

23. Favourite Things

Come watch my favourite movie,
You promised me you'd do it,
Feels like ages since you said to me,
For me, you'll sit right through it.

I waited for the day to come,
It was too good to be true,
I'm tired of waiting, I'm done,
So today I watched it without you.

I'm sorry, but I waited for so long,
I waited till I lost all hope,
I waited, cried and wrote songs,
I waited, but you're still a ghost.

Maybe you would've found it fine,
If you were you, you'd look at me,
Your arm would be entangled in mine,
And your eyes won't watch the screen.

But your ghost is by my side,
And it's not half as warm as you,
Its arms are by its sides,
On the screen, its eyes are glued.

So now I'm aware that I'm all alone,
And that something is missing,
So, it was that easy for you to go,
You ruined two of my favourite things.

24. The things I did

The things I did you to call you mine,
Embarrass me from time to time,
The corny poems and childish words,
Can't overshadow how much love hurts.

The things I did to call this "us",
Remind me of how I could never be enough,
Because I'm flawed, but so are you,
Then why does only my heart seem so blue?

The things I did to make believe,
That your puzzle was my mystery,
Have left me in pieces myself,
With broken corners that have bled.

The things I did to hold on to you,
A broken record stuck on loop,
The lyrics blur, but I'm used to it,
This broken love got addicting.

The things I'll do to forget your smile,
To find someone else to spend my life,
Shall fill the voids my soul has felt,
Your apathy has never helped.

The things I'll do to heal from love,
The wounds in salt I cover up,
With bandaids of the words I think,
Until I'm consumed by everything.

25. The epilogue you don't deserve

You pointed the shining blade at me,
And in loving you, I told you where to cut.
Maybe bleeding for you was destiny,
But I could control it, and not my love.

Promise me you'll walk away with a smile
I'd hate to believe I ruined everything,
I'll let you blame me yes, I'm that blind,
To let you believe I was worth nothing.

You were good, I'll convince myself for us both,
Despite my arm spilling blood on the floor,
I can see your footprints fade into the unknown,
To remind you, my blood holds onto your toes.

But just before you disappear, I see you kick,
I see you try to get rid of every bit of me,
But even in my pain, I hear your brown eyes blink,
You're just acting, I can hear your breath watching me.

Do you watch me because you enjoy my pain?
Or is it because you actually have some shame?

I'd bleed for anything that held my arms today,
Why take me for granted? You promised you'd stay.

26. Biggest Masochist

With the frigid ocean numbing my feet,
And the sea salt gnawing at my eyes,
With the need for an answer playing on repeat,
I dared to question the sky.

The drunk lovers resort to the bottles of wine,
To drown their feelings with the blood of pleasure,
The anxious girls in their bedroom at night,
Let the blade run on their skin under pressure.

The tall children in the bodies of men,
Who smile through the pain of leaving home,
The tales of heroic, abandoned women,
Who worked for what they own.

"Who's the biggest masochist in this broken world?",
A storm was in the making, as the moon would reply,
Was it the echo of my words that left me shaking?
Or the answer I was to find?

The thunder growled and responded,
I had always dreaded these words,
"The poets like you," I was astonished,
I smiled as my insides hurt.

"You bleed your pieces on to paper,
To comfort the ones in need,
The creed that could never have a hater,
You're the epitome of insanity.

To comfort the world, you break your soul,
Ripping your hearts out to feed them to all,
You're the escapism for the mortals in this hole,
Yet your puzzle pieces are always unsolved.

You hurt yourself and smile through it,
You stare at your broken soul in pride,
Who is a bigger masochist than you,
When you ask for answers you wouldn't like?"